Benjamin Harrison

☆ ☆ ☆

Benjamin Harrison

Jean Kinney Williams

AMERICA'S
23RD
PRESIDENT

Children's Press®
A Division of Scholastic Inc.
New York / Toronto / London / Auckland / Sydney
Mexico City / New Delhi / Hong Kong
Danbury, Connecticut

Library of Congress Cataloging-in-Publication Data

Williams, Jean Kinney.
      Benjamin Harrison / by Jean Kinney Williams.
         p. cm. — (Encyclopedia of presidents)
      Includes bibliographical references (p.   ) and index.
   ISBN 0-516-22959-1
   1. Harrison, Benjamin, 1833–1901—Juvenile literature. 2. Presidents—
United States—Biography—Juvenile literature. I. Title. II. Series.
E702.W55 2004
973.8'6'092—dc22   2004000132

CHILDREN'S PRESS and associated logos are trademarks and or registered
trademarks of Scholastic Library Publishing. SCHOLASTIC and associated
logos are trademarks and or registered trademarks of Scholastic Inc.
1 2 3 4 5 6 7 8 9 10 R 13 12 11 10 09 08 07 06 05 04

Contents

Chapter 1

Grandson of a President

"Tippecanoe and Tyler, Too!"

In the summer of 1840, when young Benjamin Harrison turned seven years old, his family and his neighbors in North Bend, Ohio, were in a dither of excitement. The Whig party had nominated Benjamin's grandfather, William Henry Harrison, to run for president. Through the summer and fall, the Whigs carried on one of the most colorful campaigns in history. They sponsored parades and meetings for Harrison in every town and village. William Henry Harrison was known as "Old Tippecanoe" for a victory he had won as an army commander against Native Americans at Tippecanoe Creek in Indiana. The Whig campaign slogan rang out across the country. "Tippecanoe and Tyler, Too!" crowds chanted, urging everyone to vote for Harrison and his vice-presidential running mate John Tyler.

As a favorite grandson, Benjamin must have been excited and pleased by the campaign for his grandfather. That fall, William Henry Harrison was elected to the presidency. In February 1841, he left North Bend to take office in Washington, D.C. He took the oath of office on March 4, and delivered an inauguration speech that lasted an hour and forty minutes.

Benjamin never got a chance to visit his grandfather in the White House. Only weeks after he became president, William Henry Harrison fell ill with pneumonia, and on April 4, he died. Young Benjamin must also have remembered the day that spring when his grandfather's body was brought back to North Bend for burial.

In 1889, just 48 years after his grandfather was sworn in as president, Benjamin Harrison himself took the same oath of office. As a young man, he disliked being reminded of his famous grandfather. Still, his grandfather's success gave Harrison a sense of confidence. As he rose in politics, he was one man who never found it surprising or amazing that he might be elected to the highest office in the land.

Early Life

Benjamin Harrison was born August 20, 1833, at North Bend, Ohio, on the Ohio River west of Cincinnati, in the home of his illustrious grandfather. He was at least the sixth son in the Harrison family to be named Benjamin. The first Benjamin arrived in the American colony of Virginia from England in the 1630s. The fifth Benjamin Harrison (young Benjamin's great-grandfather) was a prosperous planter who served 27 years in Virginia's colonial legislature, was a signer of the Declaration of Independence, and served as Virginia's governor after the Revolutionary War.

William Henry Harrison was a younger son of the fifth Benjamin. He became an army officer and gained fame for his victory at Tippecanoe and for later victories against the British in Canada during the War of 1812. He settled on 2,000 acres (800 hectares) of land in North Bend, where he became a gentleman farmer and a political leader.

Benjamin's father, John Scott Harrison, was one of William Henry Harrison's sons. He received several hundred acres of his father's land and settled down to farm. He married and had two daughters, but then his wife died. Later he married Elizabeth Irwin of Pennsylvania. Benjamin was their second son. In addition to Benjamin and his older brother Irwin, the Harrisons had several more children, four of whom survived infancy. His mother, Elizabeth Harrison, was a devout and active Presbyterian and raised her children in that faith.

Growing up on the Point, as John Scott Harrison's farm was called, Benjamin enjoyed his life of farm chores, attending a log cabin school, and especially fishing in the Ohio River and hunting along its banks. From the family's front porch Benjamin could watch flatboats and steamships heading down the river as settlers continued to push the frontier west.

The Harrison family grew much of its own food. Elizabeth and her daughters made most of the family's clothing. John Scott Harrison earned just enough money to hold onto his land and educate his children. Nevertheless, John Scott

Benjamin Harrison was born on this farm in North Bend, Ohio, a few miles from the home of his grandfather, William Henry Harrison.

and Elizabeth Harrison were loving and encouraging parents. Later, when he was away at school, Benjamin looked forward to visits home for the Christmas holiday or to help with plowing and harvesting on the farm.

When Benjamin was 14, he and his brother Irwin were sent to a boarding school in Cincinnati. Like other schoolboys of the day, they studied mathematics, science, Latin, philosophy, and religion. One of his teachers was John Scott, a Presbyterian minister. Scott had an attractive daughter named Caroline (or Carrie), with whom Ben struck up a friendship.

Benjamin showed great promise as a student, and his father hoped to send him to an eastern college such as Yale. In the summer of 1850, however, Benjamin's mother died at the age of 40. Benjamin's father was left to provide for four sons and two daughters ranging in age from 6 to 18. He decided that Benjamin should study closer to home, and sent him to Miami University, a publicly supported college in Oxford, Ohio, about 40 miles (64 kilometers) from North Bend.

Finding a Career and a Wife ———————

In 1850 Benjamin enrolled at Miami as a third-year student. His former teacher, John Scott, had recently moved to Oxford to establish a new college for women, and Benjamin was soon courting Scott's daughter Carrie. She was a student at

Harrison studied at Miami University in Oxford, Ohio. It was supported by the state of Ohio, but it also served as a training school for Presbyterian ministers.

her father's new college and also taught music there. Benjamin paid frequent visits to the Scott home in Oxford to spend time with her. Sometimes the couple sneaked out for carriage rides and even dances, which were frowned on by her family.

In 1852 Benjamin graduated from Miami and Carrie graduated from her father's college. During his college years, Benjamin considered entering the Presbyterian ministry, but decided instead to study law. He and Carrie had also discussed marriage, but that would have to wait until he was able to make a living to support her. He went to Cincinnati to serve as an unpaid apprentice in a law firm, studying under one of the attorneys there. He lived with his older half-sister Elizabeth (Bessie) and her young family. Carrie went to Carrollton, Kentucky, to teach in a girls' school.

In Cincinnati, Benjamin drove himself to study long hours. In a letter to his sister Anna, he wrote, "I do the same things every day. . . . Eat three meals . . . sleep six hours and read dusty old books." In the meantime, he missed Carrie and waited eagerly for her letters from Carrollton. Local post office workers chuckled at the lovesick young man who came in every day to ask for his mail. Harrison also found he didn't like living in the bustling city. In another letter home, he said he longed for "green grass and fresh air."

In the fall of 1853, Benjamin and Carrie decided to marry, even though he was not yet earning a living. They could live with his family in North Bend while he finished his studies. Carrie's father, Dr. Scott, performed the wedding at the Scott home in Oxford on October 20, 1853.

After his marriage, Benjamin continued to spend long hours with his law books, but he was much happier. He wrote to his friend John Anderson, "Her presence and the consciousness that she is my wife . . . afford an infinitude of quiet happiness." Carrie helped care for the younger Harrison children during her stay in North Bend. Ben's father had been elected to the U.S. House of Representatives, and that fall he left for Washington, D.C., to take up his duties.

Indianapolis

In 1854 Benjamin passed the Ohio law exam and was licensed to practice. Since he had been unhappy in the industrial city of Cincinnati, he decided he would set up practice somewhere farther west. He considered Chicago, but finally settled on Indianapolis, the capital of Indiana. His cousin William Sheets, a successful businessman in Indianapolis, encouraged the Harrisons to come, offering them a temporary place to stay.

Harrison looked forward to getting a start in Indianapolis. It was still a small city, but it was growing rapidly. As the capital of Indiana, it was at the center of the state's political and legal system. In addition, his family name was nearly as well known in Indiana as it was around Cincinnati. His grandfather had served as a governor of the Indiana Territory and had won his famous victory at Tippecanoe there. Perhaps another attraction was that Indianapolis was only about 75 miles (120 km) from the old homestead at North Bend.

Chapter 2

A Young Lawyer's Struggles ——————

Benjamin and Carrie Harrison arrived in Indianapolis in April 1854, carrying all their belongings in one large box. The first months in their adopted city were difficult. Benjamin had to build a law practice from scratch, and for a time he had difficulty finding work. The couple shared a house with another family, the Kitchens. Many years later, John Kitchen remembered Benjamin Harrison as "kindly, agreeable and studious, reserved even then, but attracting persons to him by his intellectual qualities." Kitchen added that Harrison "made a success of everything he undertook."

One day during that first year, the house burned to the ground, leaving Benjamin and Carrie homeless. To make matters worse, Carrie was expecting their first child. They decided that she should return to Oxford, where her family could care for her after the baby

When Benjamin and Carrie Harrison came to Indianapolis in 1854, they lived near Pennsylvania Street, shown here.

was born. Meanwhile, Benjamin lived in inexpensive rooms and doubled his effort to find new law clients. He rented a small office in a bank building and found a temporary job at the federal courthouse that paid $2.50 a day, then a fairly large sum.

Harrison's first court case was tried in the backyard of a justice of the peace 10 miles (16 km) outside the city, and he was paid $5 for his services.

Later, he became an assistant to the city *prosecutor*, who brought charges against those accused of criminal offenses. Harrison had the job of making the closing argument for the prosecution at trial. In one outdoor trial, darkness was falling as Harrison stood up to make his argument. Unable to read his notes, Harrison put them aside and summarized the evidence from memory, winning a guilty verdict from the jury. He was always willing to research his cases thoroughly. In one trial of a man accused of killing another by poison, he stayed up all night learning about different poisons. The next day, his informed questions helped win the case.

The Harrisons' first child, Russell, was born in Oxford in August 1854. Weeks later, Carrie returned to Indianapolis with the baby. Through the winter, Benjamin struggled to earn enough to keep the family together. In January 1855, he was down to his last $2. Finally, as spring approached, things began to look up. In March he was invited to join the successful law practice of William Wallace. From this point on, Harrison's talent and his hard work set him on the road to success.

A Start in Politics

Even as the young Harrison family was struggling, so was the United States. The question about whether the new territories in the West should allow slavery or prohibit it had become so bitter that it was dividing the country. Citizens in the South defended slavery and insisted that southerners who moved west should be able to take their slaves with them. Many in the North were dead set against the spread of slavery beyond the states where it currently was allowed. In fact, a growing faction known as *abolitionists* wanted to abolish, or end, slavery altogether.

The dispute divided both political parties. The old Whig party, which had elected William Henry Harrison, was so split that it went out of existence. In the meantime, northerners who opposed the spread of slavery began to form the new Republican party. Restricting slavery was their main issue, but they also favored support by the *federal* (or national) government for improvements such as roads.

Young Benjamin Harrison was drawn to the new party and began attending its meetings in Indianapolis. In 1856 he campaigned for John C. Frémont, the Republicans' first presidential candidate. Frémont lost to Democrat James Buchanan, but many Republican candidates were elected to Congress and to state offices. Harrison's father was dismayed that his son had become a Republican. John Scott Harrison, who had lived just across the Ohio River from the slave state of Kentucky for most of his life, believed that slavery should be tolerated in order to preserve the country. From this point on, Benjamin and his father often disagreed over politics, but their disagreements did not end their affection for each other.

JNº C. FREMONT.   Wᵐ L. DAYTON.
THE CHAMPIONS OF FREEDOM.

In 1856, young Benjamin Harrison campaigned for John C. Frémont, the presidential candidate of the newly formed Republican party.

Living Up to the Family Name

It wasn't always easy to be a Harrison. Having a famous name probably helped Benjamin Harrison's career many times, but sometimes it caused him embarrassment. One day during the campaign in 1856, several Republicans burst into his law office and asked him to come out and make a speech as the grandson of President William Henry Harrison.

Harrison protested that he wasn't ready to give a speech, but the men half-carried him to the campaign platform and introduced him as the former president's grandson. When the crowd finished cheering, young Harrison said, "I want it understood that I am the grandson of nobody. I believe that every man should stand on his own merits." Then he went on to speak in favor of the Republican candidates.

☆ ☆ ☆

In 1857 Harrison ran for Indianapolis city attorney and was elected. He believed strongly that citizens should be willing to serve the community, but he also realized that public office could help him succeed as a lawyer. He remained active in party affairs, becoming secretary of the Republican state central committee in 1858. This position gave him a chance to meet Republicans from many parts of the state and to get familiar with the way candidates were nominated and elected to higher offices. That same year, the Harrisons welcomed a daughter, Mary (whom they called Mamie).

Harrison began exploring opportunities in the state legal system. In 1860 he ran for state supreme court reporter. The reporter was responsible for summarizing and printing the decisions of the state supreme court. The summaries were bound into books and sold to lawyers, and the reporter's income came from the sale of the books. Because every law firm in the state needed these records, the supreme court reporter earned a handsome income.

Harrison and the other candidates campaigned through the state in the fall of 1860. It was an important political year, filled with debate about slavery. Abraham Lincoln, the Republican candidate for president, was popular among Republicans because of his firm views against the spread of slavery, but he was despised by proslavery Democrats. Indiana voters were divided. Many in the southern part of the state had come from Kentucky and felt close to the South. Harrison was advised to go easy on his views against slavery when he campaigned in the southern part of the state, but he refused. He prepared a single set of speaking notes and gave the same speech north and south, opposing the spread of slavery and supporting Abraham Lincoln.

When Harrison stopped to campaign in Rockville, he learned that Democratic candidates, including Thomas Hendricks, the party's nominee for governor, were scheduled to speak that night, leaving little chance for Harrison to make his case. A gathering crowd of Democrats and Republicans called for a debate between the experienced Hendricks and Harrison, who was only 27 years old and running for a minor office. Harrison accepted the challenge. Hendricks and his supporters spoke first, taking several hours to expound their Democratic views. Harrison listened carefully. Then he stood up and refuted each of the earlier speakers' points calmly but forcefully. According to an early Harrison biography, someone in the crowd exclaimed, "What a drubbing the little fellow did give them. And he was so clean about it."

Harrison was easily elected supreme court reporter in October. Republican Oliver Morton also defeated Thomas Hendricks for governor. In November, Abraham Lincoln was elected president. Republicans were elated, but Democrats, especially in the South, were defiant. Before year's end, the first southern state *seceded* from the Union, declaring its independence from the United States. By the time Lincoln took office in March, the southern states had formed the Confederate States of America, and war was near at hand. On April 12, 1861, Confederates fired on a Union fort in South Carolina, and the Civil War began.

Meanwhile, Harrison took over his duties as supreme court reporter. President Lincoln called for volunteers to fight the Confederacy and save the Union. Indiana volunteers enlisted by the thousands. For now, Harrison would

Abraham Lincoln

Abraham Lincoln became a hero to Benjamin Harrison. In February 1861, on his way to Washington to serve as president, Lincoln stopped in Indianapolis and Harrison heard him speak. The president-elect was already weighed down by the problems of a country that was already breaking in two as states seceded from the Union. Years later, Harrison wrote, "The course before him was lighted only by the lamp of duty; outside its radiance all was dark. . . . But so strong was his sense of duty, so courageous his heart . . . that he moved forward calmly to his appointed work."

☆ ☆ ☆

stay at home with his wife and two young children. The Harrison family was also housing Harrison's younger brother and one of his nephews who had moved to Indianapolis.

As his law business increased and his court reporting responsibilities got under way, Harrison resumed his old habit of working himself to exhaustion, finding little time for his family. He hoped to buy a new home that would accommodate his growing family and relatives. His father chided him gently in a letter about his long hours. "Professional men should remember that their families have claims upon them as well as their clients," he wrote.

The Call to War ——————————————

At the beginning of the Civil War, many northerners believed that the Confederate states would be defeated in a matter of weeks or months. By the spring of 1862, however, it was clear that the war would be long and bitter. Union armies had suffered serious defeats at Bull Run and Ball's Bluff in Virginia. Then in April 1862, a northern force led by Ulysses S. Grant narrowly avoided defeat at Shiloh in Tennessee. In two days of fighting, the two armies suffered 23,000 men killed, wounded, or missing. Later that spring, the Confederates won more victories in Virginia. In July President Lincoln asked northern states to recruit 300,000 more soldiers. Benjamin Harrison decided to enlist. His law practice and his new house would have to wait.

On a hot mid-August day Colonel Benjamin Harrison and his regiment, the 70th Indiana, left Indianapolis, bound for Kentucky. After a long march, they arrived in Bowling Green where they drilled and trained for battle. Colonel Harrison was as new to the army as the young men he commanded, so after a day of drilling his new recruits, he spent the evening studying military tactics. He always found time to write letters home to Carrie, as well.

Just as he expected much of himself, Harrison expected much from his men. Major Samuel Merrill, who kept the regiment's history, wrote that "discipline was severe" under Harrison, who "knew that without discipline a thousand

Harrison enlisted in the Union army in 1862. He was 29 years old.

men are no better than a mob." Harrison's goal was to create "a battalion that in the day of battle would move as if animated by one soul," Merrill wrote. When whiskey became a problem, Harrison banned it. Harrison was not popular among his men, but he had their respect, and his high expectations would pay off when the regiment was put to the test.

Harrison's regiment was sent out on a few missions to catch Confederate raiders, who were destroying railroad tracks and bridges. On one such mission, Harrison led 600 men to Russellville, Kentucky. On the way they had a chance skirmish with Confederates, who lost 35 men while Harrison lost only one. They found no raiders in Russellville, however, and returned to their base.

Back in Indianapolis, a Democrat was elected as supreme court reporter in the fall of 1862, depriving Harrison of his office. He was also discouraged by the letters his men were receiving from home, encouraging them to leave the army. Not all northerners supported the war, and "Copperheads," or antiwar Democrats, used news of Union army losses to stir up resentment against the war.

In November, Harrison's regiment was ordered to Gallatin, Tennessee. By now, they were hoping to see action soon. Once again, they were disappointed. In late December, large Union and Confederate armies engaged in battle at Stones River, near Murfreesboro. Harrison and his men were still guarding the railroad, far from the fighting. As winter's chill set in, the 70th Indiana battled cold and boredom.

Harrison's letters to Carrie were warm and expressive. In a Christmas Eve 1862 letter he envisioned their children, "filled with high expectations of what Santa Claus will bring them, and Papa is not there." He said that he understood he was only one of thousands of men longing for home and family, and he thanked Carrie "for the heroic spirit with which you bear our separation . . . and its hardships."

Leading Troops in Battle

The 70th Indiana continued to perform minor duties through 1863 and early 1864, never participating in a major fight. During that time, however, Union forces had begun

Fast Facts
THE CIVIL WAR

Who: The United States (the Union, or the North) against the Confederate States of America, made up of southern states that had seceded from the Union

When: April 12, 1861–May 1865

Why: Southern states, believing the election of Abraham Lincoln threatened states' rights and slavery, seceded from the United States and fought for their independence. The North fought to restore the southern states to the Union, and later to end slavery.

Where: States along the border between the Union and the Confederacy, especially Virginia and Tennessee. Confederate forces had early successes, but were overcome by the Union's superior resources. Major northern victories came at Gettysburg, Pennsylvania, and Vicksburg, Mississippi (both July 1863); Atlanta, Georgia (September 1864); and Petersburg and Richmond, Virginia (both April 1865).

Outcome: The Confederate Army of Northern Virginia surrendered to Union forces April 9, 1865, ending the major fighting. The victorious North passed legislation that abolished slavery, gave civil rights to former slaves, and put defeated states under military rule.

to defeat the Confederacy with major victories at Gettysburg, Pennsylvania; Vicksburg, Mississippi; and Chattanooga, Tennessee. The 70th Indiana was assigned to one of the armies at Chattanooga under the command of General William Tecumseh Sherman. His job was to pursue the Confederate army into Georgia. Now Harrison and his troops would make up for the long months of inaction.

Beginning on May 13, 1864, the Union army was locked in a hard struggle with Confederate forces for Resaca, a small town between Chattanooga and Atlanta. Harrison and his men were fighting under the command of General Joseph "Fighting Joe" Hooker. After two days of fierce fighting, the Union had not been able to take control of the city. Harrison knew that on May 15, his troops would see real battle for the first time. The night before, he wrote to Carrie, "I am thinking much of you and the dear children and my whole heart comes out towards you in tenderness and love and many earnest prayers will I send up to God this night, should you lose a husband and they a father."

The next day, Harrison received the order to attack a Confederate force well protected by a swampy ravine and a thickly wooded hill. He was to lead his men down into the ravine and up to the hilltop. Afterward he wrote to Carrie that he waved his cap and "cheered the men on" as they ran uphill together into a storm of bullets. His men, Harrison wrote, "moved on with perfect steadiness" right up to the line of fire, even as soldiers fell around them. All the months of drilling were now paying off.

Harrison's charge was a bright spot in a battle won by neither side. The Confederate forces finally retreated when Union troops march south beyond Resaca, threatening their lines of supply. General Hooker complimented Harrison on a "very brilliant charge." Harrison was also pleased to win his men's admiration. "I have got to love them for their bravery and for dangers we have shared together," he wrote later.

As the Union army pushed the Confederates nearer to Atlanta, Harrison was in the thick of battle with his men at New Hope Church, and at Golgotha Church in June. The regiment experienced heavy losses. Army doctors became separated from the troops during the June battle, and after spending a day in combat, Harrison tended to his injured men, dressing their wounds as well as he could.

By July, the Union army was closing in on Atlanta. The Confederates retreated across Peach Tree Creek, a small creek running east to west, only three miles from the city. The Union Army of the Cumberland (which included Harrison's troops) followed across the creek and took up defensive positions. Harrison's brigade settled into a hollow, and he rode his horse up a small hill to study the situation. He was surprised to find an unguarded gap along a quarter-mile stretch of the hilltop, a perfect spot for Confederates to push through Union

At the battle of Resaca in 1864 (above), Harrison led his troops on a "very brilliant charge" against Confederates who held the hill in the background. Soon afterward, an artist portrayed Harrison leading the attack (right), shouting, "Come on, boys!"

lines. Before he could remedy the situation, the Confederate army made its first attack on the unprotected hill. Harrison ordered his men to the hill, and soon they were in hand-to-hand combat with Confederate soldiers, too close to fire their rifles and muskets. After a bloody fight, the Confederates withdrew. Harrison's men gained credit for helping to stop this first attack. General Hooker recommended Harrison for promotion to brigadier general for his services that day.

War's End

Soon after the battle, Harrison received a leave to return to Indianapolis, where he was needed for the fall political campaign. He helped organize support in Indiana for President Lincoln and Governor Morton, who were running for re-election, and he ran again for supreme court reporter. All three, Lincoln, Morton, and Harrison, were elected. In his victory speech, Harrison blasted the antiwar Copperheads and praised the help and work of the African Americans who were fighting for the Union.

Before he could return to his unit in Georgia, Harrison was ordered to lead a brigade in the Union army defending Nashville, Tennessee, against Confederate attack. The armies met south of the city in mid-December, and the Union army scored a major victory. Harrison then rejoined the 70th Indiana, which had marched across Georgia to Savannah with General Sherman's army and would

In December 1864, Harrison took part in a major Union victory at Nashville, Tennessee. In this photograph, Union troops are camped on a rise overlooking Confederate positions.

soon invade South Carolina. Confederate forces were on the run. In early April, the Union army captured Richmond, Virginia, the Confederate capital, and soon afterward, Confederate general Robert E. Lee surrendered to Union general Ulysses S. Grant. Smaller Confederate forces surrendered in the following weeks, and the war came to an end.

Chapter 3

Peacetime

In April 1865, only days after the Confederate armies in Virginia surrendered, President Abraham Lincoln was assassinated (shot and
killed), leaving the people and armies of the Union to celebrate victory and mourn the death of a president at the same time. Vice
President Andrew Johnson was sworn in as the new president.

In May the armies of the Union gathered in Washington, D.C.,
to stage a giant "Grand Review" before they returned to their homes.
For two long days, they paraded past cheering crowds. The president
and his cabinet viewed the parade from a special reviewing stand.
Harrison's 70th Indiana paraded with all the others. General William
Tecumseh Sherman told the troops, "As in war you have been good
soldiers, so in peace you will make good citizens."

Together with thousands of others, Benjamin Harrison, now 31 years old, returned to civilian life, changed by his wartime experience. He would never forget the men with whom he had faced near-death, or those they had buried after battle. Yet he had gained a new sense of personal command, and he formed a lasting bond with the men who fought with him. He remained a staunch supporter of Civil War veterans for the rest of his life.

Like other returning veterans, Harrison was also determined to make up for lost time. For three years his family had made do with his soldier's salary, and they were still living in crowded conditions. His son Russell was now eleven and Mamie was seven. He still helped support his younger brothers, and his older brother Irwin was ill with tuberculosis. (Benjamin Harrison was grief-stricken when Irwin finally died in 1870.)

Harrison promised Carrie that now he would pay more attention to his family, but once again he was soon buried in work. He took up his duties as supreme court reporter and redoubled his efforts to increase his law practice. Before long, he collapsed from exhaustion. He decided not to run again for supreme court reporter and concentrated on practicing law.

Even though he was out of office, Harrison continued to participate in Republican politics. The disputes after the war were nearly as heated at those before it began. Harrison stood with the "Radical" Republicans. He believed that the southern states must be forced to grant rights to African Americans, even if this required use of federal troops. He believed that former slaves should receive better education and that they should become full citizens with the right to participate in government and vote in elections. In 1866 Radical Republicans swept the congressional elections, winning majorities in the Congress that would dictate harsh "Reconstruction" policies in the South. In 1868, Ulysses S. Grant, who had been the leading Union general, was elected president with the support of the Radicals.

The Milligan Case

Harrison's activity in Republican affairs helped his law firm gain an important assignment from the Grant administration. He was asked to defend the government and Union officers in Indiana against a suit brought by Lambdin Milligan.

Milligan, an Indiana resident, had been an antiwar Democrat and a member of the Sons of Liberty, a secret society that supported the Confederacy. He was captured and put on trial by a military commission, convicted of treason, and sent to prison in Ohio. Milligan sued, claiming that the military commission had no right to try him and that any trial should have been in a regular civilian court. In 1866, the U.S. Supreme Court supported his claim, and Milligan was freed.

In 1871 Milligan brought suit against the officers who had tried and convicted him, seeking damages of $100,000 for his improper conviction and imprisonment. His lawyer was Thomas Hendricks, the Democratic candidate Harrison had debated years earlier in Rockville. The Grant administration asked Harrison to defend the officers and the government.

Harrison knew Milligan had a good case, but he presented a strong case for the officers as well. He reminded the jury of the dangerous wartime conditions in Indiana and emphasized the patriotism of the officers who convicted Milligan. In addition, he revealed the treasonous activities that Milligan had supported and pointed out that Milligan refused to fight in a war to preserve the Constitution, but was now claiming its protection. The jury's decision provided victory of sorts for each side. It ruled in favor of Milligan and against the government, but it awarded Milligan only $5 in damages. Harrison's skilled defense of the Union officers gained him wide support and praise in Indiana.

Republican Troubles

As Harrison worked hard in Indiana courtrooms, the Republican administration in Washington was coming under a cloud. It had broad support throughout the northern states, not only from citizens, but also from ambitious business leaders. Many of these leaders did business with the government and were eager to find ways to increase their profits. During Grant's eight years as president, many learned to gain government contracts by paying bribes to government officials. Others tried to manipulate government policies to gain grants of land and other favors. Grant himself was honest, but it soon became clear that his Republican appointees and friends were taking advantage of their positions to get rich at the government's expense. Some were becoming millionaires.

In 1872 Benjamin Harrison was frequently mentioned as a candidate for governor, but he would not publicly pursue the nomination. It went instead to Tom Browne, who lost the election to Harrison's old adversary, Democrat Thomas Hendricks. Harrison may have had mixed feelings about running for office, since he continued to be concerned about family finances. On the other hand, he may have been more ambitious than he appeared to be, working behind the scenes but failing to gain the nomination.

A serious depression in 1873–74 caused widespread suffering throughout the country, but Harrison and his firm continued to prosper. In 1875 the Harrisons built a spacious new home on North Delaware Street, realizing a longtime dream. Now they had ample room in the new house to entertain social gatherings and church groups. Harrison also had an office, where he could meet with clients and prepare cases. Today the house serves as a museum that recalls the life and times of the 23rd president.

In 1875 Harrison built a new house for his family on North Delaware Street in Indianapolis. He later spent years in Washington and elsewhere, but this remained his permanent home for the rest of his life.

A Race for Governor

In 1876 Harrison was once again mentioned as a candidate for governor, but he refused to pursue the nomination actively. Republicans nominated former Congressman Godlove Orth to run against Democrat James "Blue Jeans" Williams. True to his nickname, Williams, a tall, homely man who reminded people of Abraham Lincoln, campaigned in denim trousers.

During the campaign, it was revealed that Republican candidate Orth had been involved in political corruption, and he was forced to quit the race. Even though Harrison had expressed little interest, the Republicans took a chance and

The Bloody Shirt

Like other Republicans at the time, Harrison effectively used the campaign tactic called "waving the bloody shirt." In many campaigns after the Civil War, a Republican candidate actually held up the bloodstained shirt of a Union soldier to remind the crowd that Republicans had supported the war to preserve the Union, while Democrats were associated with rebels and traitors from the South. As a war hero with close ties to veterans' groups, Harrison was in a good position to remind voters that Republicans were patriots who helped win the war.

☆☆☆

nominated him. This time he accepted. The Democratic campaign immediately branded him the "kid-glove" candidate, contrasting him to the folksy "Blue Jeans" Williams. (Gloves made of fine leather from a young goat were expensive and worn only by prosperous people.)

Harrison's stirring speeches could sway a crowd or jury, but in closer contact with people he often seemed aloof and cold. He also had to fight the Republicans' growing reputation for corruption. Across the nation, Democrats were gaining strength as Republicans struggled.

The election for governor was so close that it took three days after the election to determine a winner. In the end, Williams won by 5,000 votes, and Harrison returned to his law practice. Still, the campaign helped raise his political stature as a leader of Indiana's Republican party.

Labor

In 1877 a nationwide railroad strike broke out. Railroad workers in the East had received a pay cut and walked off the job. Soon other railway workers across the country walked out in sympathy. There were bloody clashes between strikers and state militias from Baltimore to San Francisco.

In July Indianapolis railroad workers also left their jobs, disconnected railroad cars, and seized the train depot. Another battle between strikers and local authorities seemed unavoidable, but Governor Williams refused to take action. Benjamin Harrison and other city leaders organized a volunteer citizens' group to keep order. He also helped establish a special committee to hear complaints from the strikers and the railroad owners. Harrison advised the strikers to return to work, obey the law, and allow the committee to work for pay raises on their behalf. Violence was avoided, and many Indianapolis residents saw Harrison as a true leader.

Later that year, Senator Oliver Morton died. Morton, who had also served as governor, had been Harrison's main competitor in Republican politics, and his death left Harrison as the state's most prominent Republican. In 1879, President Rutherford B. Hayes appointed Harrison to the Mississippi River Commission, a newly organized group with responsibility to survey the great river and find ways to improve navigation and protect against disastrous flooding. Harrison was the only one of the seven-member commission who was not an army officer or an engineer.

Senator Harrison

In 1880, Harrison campaigned energetically for the election of James Garfield to the presidency. Soon after the election, Garfield offered Harrison a cabinet position. Harrison turned down the offer, deciding instead to run for the U.S. Senate from

As Benjamin Harrison rose in national politics, the most famous and admired American writer of the day was Mark Twain (1835–1910). He was about the same age as Harrison, and for years he had kept the country laughing with his short sketches about life in the West, accounts of his own experiences, and his novels.

In 1872 Twain had written a book called *The Gilded Age*, which was about the period he and the United States were living through. It made fun of its characters' behavior, especially the behavior of the rich. In the Gilded Age, Twain wrote with a wink, "the chief aim of man is to get rich . . . dishonestly if we can; honestly if we must." His readers understood that a gilded object was one made of inexpensive material but covered with a thin, shiny coat of gold to make it look rich and desirable.

Mark Twain, America's leading writer and humorist, described the era as "the Gilded Age." His readers understood that a gilded object has a thin shiny coat of gold but is really made of cheap metal.

Twain's humor helped him express his anger and indignation about those who were willing to get rich dishonestly, including corrupt politicians in the Grant administration, bankers and businessmen who cheated the public, and employers who exploited and underpaid their workers. He was quietly urging his readers to demand honesty and reform in business and in politics. Even today, the period between the Civil War and 1900 is often called the Gilded Age. Harrison and his presidency were part of it.

Indiana. At the time, U.S. senators were elected by state legislatures, and in January 1881, the Indiana legislature elected Harrison for a full six-year term. By this time, Harrison's financial problems were in the past. His children were adults, and his law practice had made him one of the most prosperous men in Indiana. He was free to leave his law practice and represent the people of Indiana in the Senate.

During his first year in the Senate, Harrison sat back, listened, and learned. He was amazed when hundreds of people came to ask him for appointments to government jobs. In his first experience as a member of a lawmaking body, he was also disappointed to see that quarreling and political maneuvering took up much of the Senate's time. He came to realize, as he told a friend, that he didn't have "a good stomach for a row," finding himself uncomfortable during hard bargaining to pass or block legislation.

As he grew more comfortable in the Senate, Harrison became a passionate supporter of pensions for Civil War veterans. In 1884 Democrat Grover Cleveland was elected president, and he refused to sign hundreds of "private bills" passed by the Senate to provide pensions to individuals whom he accused of lying about their war injuries. In support of the thousands of honest veterans, Harrison took one of these cases and made it a national issue in 1886.

When Cleveland took office, many Republican workers in the government lost their jobs to Democrats. One of these was the widow of a war veteran in

The Capitol Building in 1885 on an evening when Congress is meeting late. The U.S. Senate and House of Representatives meet in the Capitol.

southern Indiana who lost her post office job. Using his best oratorical skills, Harrison read a letter to the Senate from the widow, who now had no way to support herself. It was a "national disgrace," she wrote, that the government her husband died defending now robbed his widow of her financial support. Harrison's speech became national news, and was widely reprinted.

Tariffs were a major source of disagreement between Democrats and Republicans. Harrison and most other Republicans claimed that these taxes on goods imported to the United States protected American business and workers by encouraging people to buy products made at home. If cheap foreign goods were allowed, they said, American businesses might fail, and workers would lose their jobs. President Cleveland and other Democrats believed that high tariffs allowed American businesses to charge high prices because they did not have foreign competition. He claimed that lower tariffs would lead to lower prices. Cleveland tried to lower tariffs, but Republicans in Congress opposed him at every turn.

In the 1884 election, Democrats not only won the White House but also elected many candidates for state offices. In Indiana, Democrats took control of the state legislature, and they kept control in 1886. Harrison campaigned for re-election to the Senate in early 1887, but he knew that he had little chance to win. When the vote came, the Indiana legislature denied him re-election by a single vote. Later that year, he returned once more to the Harrison home on Delaware Street.

The Campaign of 1888 ——————————

As another presidential election approached, Republicans began searching for a candidate to run against Grover Cleveland. Their most influential leader was James G. Blaine, who had served as Speaker of the House of Representatives and as a senator. He had lost the 1884 election to Cleveland by a small margin, and was favored by many for the nomination. However, reform-minded Republicans were opposed to Blaine, who had been accused of corrupt dealings earlier in his career. They were seeking a fresh candidate free of any suggestion of corruption. Before the Republican nominating convention began, Blaine announced that he would not run again. "The one man . . . who in my judgment can make the best run is Benjamin Harrison," he said. Harrison's defense of high tariffs in the Senate had also gained him the support of influential businessmen.

Harrison's name was placed in nomination. On the first vote, or *ballot*, he showed strength but did not have the required majority. Finally, he won the needed votes on the eighth ballot and became the party's nominee for president. The convention nominated Levi P. Morton, a banker from New York, to run for vice president.

Like most earlier candidates for president, Cleveland did not campaign for himself. He stayed in Washington, continuing to work as president. Harrison followed the example of James Garfield, conducting his campaign from his own

Delegates to the 1888 Republican National Convention celebrate the nomination of Benjamin Harrison for president.

home in Indianapolis. Instead of traveling to bring his message to the people, he invited the public to visit him. During the summer and fall of 1888, thousands arrived in Indianapolis and gathered on Delaware Street or in a nearby park to get a glimpse of the candidate. Harrison addressed nearly 100 groups, some with as many as 2,000 people. He also met privately with important party leaders and supporters.

A broadside (left) compares the positions of Republican Harrison and Democrat Grover Cleveland in the 1888 election. A campaign poster (right) shows Harrison with his running mate Levi P. Morton. On both, Harrison supports "protection to American industry" through high tariffs.

Meanwhile, the Republican party carried on a spirited campaign for Harrison. The main theme was "protection," meaning the importance of a high tariff to protect U.S. manufacturers. The party also stood behind the gold standard for U.S. currency, a conservative policy that appealed to major businesses.

"There Can Be No Comparison...with Harrison"

One of the campaign songs sung by Republicans cheered Benjamin Harrison's record in the Civil War and criticized Grover Cleveland, who had legally paid a substitute to fight for him while he worked to support his widowed mother and younger brothers and sisters:

Oh what's the matter with Harrison?

He's all right!

There can be no comparison;

He's all right!

Ben's the man who bravely went

For his native land to shoot,

Whereas Grover Cleveland skulked

Behind the nearest substitute.

So what's the matter with Harrison?

He's all right!

☆ ☆ ☆

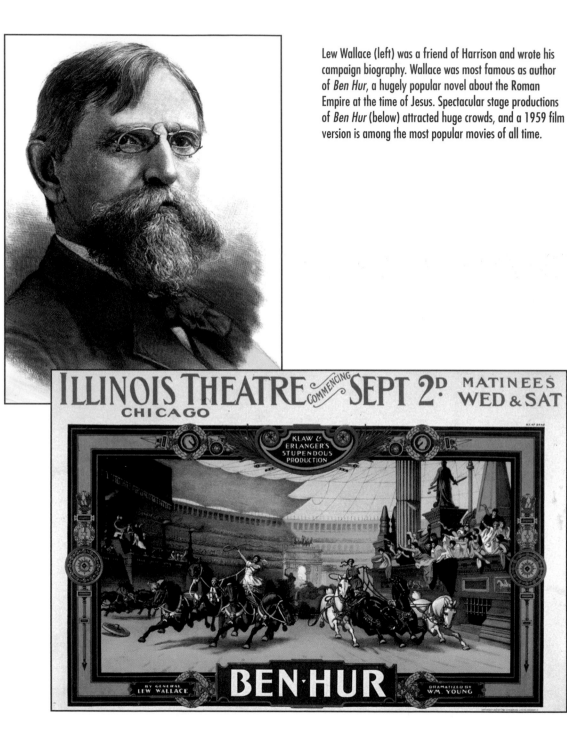

Lew Wallace (left) was a friend of Harrison and wrote his campaign biography. Wallace was most famous as author of *Ben Hur*, a hugely popular novel about the Roman Empire at the time of Jesus. Spectacular stage productions of *Ben Hur* (below) attracted huge crowds, and a 1959 film version is among the most popular movies of all time.

After voting on November 6, Harrison returned home and awaited election news on specially installed telegraph wires. On Wednesday he learned he had lost his own city of Indianapolis but narrowly won the state of Indiana. Best of all, he won Cleveland's home state of New York. In the electoral college, which actually elects the president, the winner of a state usually gets all of its electoral votes, and Harrison's victories in Indiana and New York guaranteed that he would win the presidency. Democrats were disappointed, especially because Cleveland had received about 100,000 more popular votes than Harrison, but there was no doubt about the result. Benjamin Harrison had won and would be sworn in as president in March 1889. Republicans also gained the majority of seats in the House of Representatives and held on to their majority in the Senate.

For the next four months, advice and requests poured in to Harrison—whom he should appoint to his cabinet and to other key positions, how he should deal with Congress, what positions he should take on important issues. He had to hire several secretaries to manage the bags full of mail he received each day.

Finally, on February 25, cheered on his way by a crowd of thousands, he boarded a special train headed for Washington, D.C. He bid his fellow Hoosiers what would be a temporary good-bye, saying, "I love this city." Seeming to know what lay ahead for him, he also said, "There is a great sense of loneliness in the discharge of high public duties."

Chapter 4

Appointments

The year Benjamin Harrison became the 23rd president, 1889, was the 100th anniversary of the presidency itself. George Washington had been inaugurated in 1789. It also was the 48th anniversary of the inauguration of William Henry Harrison, Benjamin's grandfather. The day dawned cold and rainy. Harrison, remembering that his grandfather had died of pneumonia only a month after taking office, took extra precautions. He wore long underwear to the outdoor ceremony. In his inaugural address, he outlined the issues most important to him: the "protective" tariff, restraining a new a business form called the "trust," taking action to combat prejudice against African Americans, strengthening America's presence in the world, and dealing with the large surplus in the U.S. Treasury.

James G. Blaine, the losing Republican candidate for president in 1884, became Benjamin Harrison's secretary of state.

Before he arrived in Washington, Harrison had decided whom to appoint to his *cabinet*, the directors of government departments that advise the president. James G. Blaine let Harrison know soon after the election that he wanted to serve as secretary of state, the cabinet member in charge of foreign affairs. Harrison planned to appoint the powerful Republican, but he did not formally offer him the position until January so that Blaine would not try to dictate his other appointments.

Other party leaders offered their advice on appointments. Harrison listened, but seemed to take little interest in the suggested candidates. His unwillingness to take advice insulted party leaders, and would later make his job as president more difficult. The two powerful Republican insiders in the cabinet were Blaine and Philadelphia businessman John Wanamaker, who had raised thousands of dollars for Harrison's campaign. Wanamaker became postmaster general, a position in which he controlled appointments to thousands of jobs in the post office and other agencies. Harrison's other appointees were less prominent Republicans whom he considered able and trustworthy.

One appointment soon ended on a sour note. Harrison chose New York corporal James Tanner, a Civil War hero who lost both legs at the second Battle of Bull Run, to be pension commissioner. Like Harrison, Tanner had a soft spot for veterans. Within a few months, however, it was obvious that many veterans were abusing the pension system, and Tanner took no action. He lacked experience in directing such a large operation, and his outspoken opinions often got him in trouble. Within six months Tanner resigned under pressure.

One lesser appointment also proved to be unpleasant. Harrison named young New York Republican Theodore Roosevelt to the Civil Service Commission, which was to police the appointment of government employees. Most commissioners did little and said less, but Roosevelt was different. A former police commissioner in New York City, he investigated suspicious appointments aggressively, and he pressured Harrison to put more government jobs under the civil service laws so that they could be filled by qualified people, not political appointees. Roosevelt complained to his friends that "the little grey man in the White House" coldly ignored or disapproved his suggestions. Harrison complained in return that young Roosevelt wanted to "put an end to all the evil in the world between sunrise and sunset." Roosevelt continued to press for reforms, and in 1901, he became the nation's 26th president.

Harrison took the job of making appointments seriously, but the stress of making so many decisions and turning down so many hopeful applicants brought out the worst of his personality traits. His personal secretary and close friend,

Harrison appointed progressive Republican Theodore Roosevelt to the U.S. Civil Service Commission. Roosevelt later served as president himself.

On April 22, 1889, thousands of land-hungry settlers raced into Oklahoma to claim former Indian land. Only 20 minutes after the first train arrived at Guthrie, they had staked out the whole town.

During Harrison's early weeks in office, part of Oklahoma (formerly Indian Territory) was opened to white settlers for the first time. The land, which had been reserved by Native Americans for hunting, was largely uninhabited. Prospective settlers were allowed to storm into the territory from bordering states at noon on April 22, 1889. They came by the thousands, by train, on horseback, and on foot, seeking promising farmland or a lot in a town. They were shocked to find that hundreds were already there, marking out towns and claiming prime locations. These "Sooners" were already waiting in line to register their claims. Many would-be settlers were disappointed. They turned around and went home, but others stayed and helped establish the new territory, which would become a state 18 years later, in 1907.

★ ★ ☆

Elijah Walker Halford, later said that he could read Harrison's moods from day to day. When Harrison greeted him, "Halford, how are you today?" Halford knew Harrison would be pleasant. On the other hand, when Harrison offered a curt "Good morning, Mr. Halford," he knew to avoid Harrison "until after lunch."

The New States

During the Cleveland administration, several territories in the West had met the qualifications for statehood, but the Democratic administration dragged its feet in admitting them. The West was largely Republican, and each new state was sure to elect two new Republican senators, who would shift the balance of power in the Senate. When Harrison was elected, the Republican-controlled Congress took swift action to admit all the eager new states. This resulted in the largest group of new states admitted during any presidential administration.

The first to be admitted were North and South Dakota, on November 2, 1889. Montana was admitted on November 8, and Washington on November 11. The following spring, Idaho and Wyoming joined the Union in May 1890, for a total of six states in just over six months. As expected, the six new states soon elected twelve new Republican senators, greatly enhancing the Republican majority in the Senate.

The States During the Presidency of Benjamin Harrison

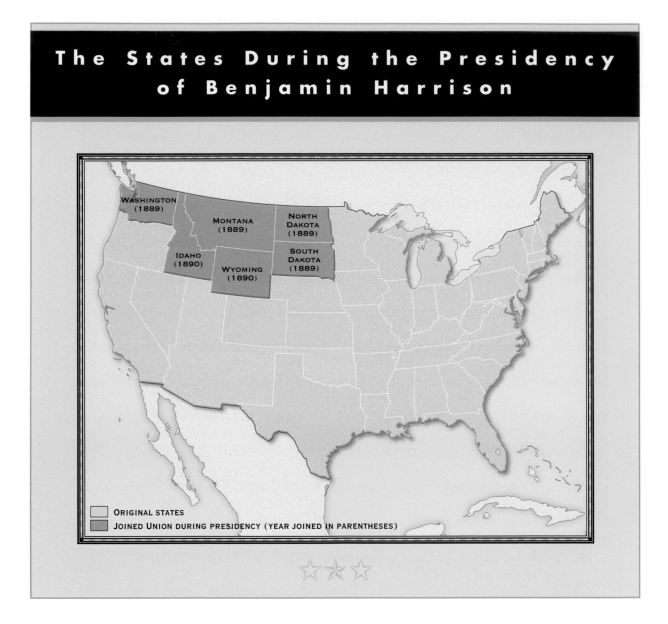

WASHINGTON
(1889)

MONTANA
(1889)

NORTH
DAKOTA
(1889)

IDAHO
(1890)

WYOMING
(1890)

SOUTH
DAKOTA
(1889)

ORIGINAL STATES

JOINED UNION DURING PRESIDENCY (YEAR JOINED IN PARENTHESES)

Trusts, Silver, and the Tariff —————

In 1890 the Republican-dominated Congress took major actions on three different fronts. The first was a reform bill designed to control the power of new business organizations called trusts. John D. Rockefeller was the major owner of companies producing and selling oil (used then mainly for lighting). These companies operated in different states and had many different functions. Some drilled for oil, some refined it, some transported it, and still others sold it to consumers. He arranged to keep control of these related companies by forming a *trust*. All the Rockefeller companies were controlled by the same small group of directors, and all their operations were managed from offices in New York. Working together, the companies could dominate the industry, drive other companies out of business, and avoid interference by any single state.

Even Republicans, who favored broad freedom for business, realized that the power of such trusts required government attention. A bill written by Ohio Senator John Sherman (brother of General William Tecumseh Sherman) outlawed some of the trusts' activities and announced that the federal government would exercise its powers to see that a trust could not take over an industry and drive all its competitors out of business. The Sherman Antitrust Act, passed in July 1890, called for fines and imprisonment for anyone trying to form a monopoly. The bill did not set aside a budget for government enforcement, however, and only one antitrust case was successfully prosecuted during Harrison's administration. Still, the act became the basis of government actions against business trusts and monopolies, and in later years it was strengthened and broadened by additional legislation.

Senator Sherman was also the main sponsor of a second bill, the Sherman Silver Purchase Act. The new legislators from the western states believed strongly that the U.S. currency system should be backed not only by gold but also by silver, which was being mined in large quantities in their region. Eastern business interests were strongly opposed to making silver a standard for currency, however. They believed U.S. currency should be backed only by gold, as it was in other important trading countries. The Silver Purchase Act offered a compromise. It required the government to buy between $2 million and $4 million in silver each month and provided for the use of silver in U.S. coins, but it did not make silver a standard for backing U.S. currency. Western legislators were unhappy with this compromise, and they later blocked other legislation backed by Harrison in retaliation.

For Republicans, the third major bill was the most important. This bill, sponsored by Ohio representative William McKinley, established a high protective

Republican Senator John Sherman of Ohio was the sponsor of the first antitrust bill passed by the U.S. Congress and of the controversial Silver Purchase Act.

tariff on nearly all goods imported into the United States. Most Republicans believed the tariff would help bring greater prosperity to business and workers alike by protecting American-made products from foreign competition. Opponents objected that other countries could impose high tariffs on American products, and that the result would be a huge reduction in world trade. To address this objection, the bill provided that the government could negotiate reciprocity agreements with other nations, in which both countries would agree to lower tariffs on particular products. The McKinley Tariff Act was passed with great fanfare in October 1890. During Harrison's administration eight reciprocity treaties were signed. Brazil, for example, agreed to open its markets to some U.S. products in exchange for lower tariffs on the coffee it exported to the United States.

Supporting African Americans

Benjamin Harrison hoped to add to these three bills a fourth piece of legislation that would protect the voting rights of African Americans in southern states. In the years since the Civil War, southern states had passed a series of laws raising requirements for voters. These laws had nearly eliminated African American voting in the South.

President Harrison had been promoting the importance of basic rights for African Americans throughout his career. "Shall the prejudices and paralysis of slavery continue to hang upon the skirts of progress?" he asked early in his presidency. In theory, voting rights for African Americans would increase votes for Republican candidates in the South, since most black voters favored the party. The bill called for the federal government to supervise all congressional elections. Republicans had a only a narrow majority in the House, and the bill passed by only a few votes. Southern Democrats condemned it, calling it the "Force Bill," suggesting the federal troops might be sent to monitor their elections.

The Senate put off discussion of the bill through 1890. Harrison tried to keep it alive by stressing its importance in his December address to Congress. When it came up for debate in early 1891, Democratic senators *filibustered* (refused to end debate and bring the bill to a vote). This tactic finally forced the Senate to table the bill without taking action, and Harrison's hopes of helping protect African American rights ended. The failure of the bill contributed to even worse conditions for African Americans in the South, and they would not win protection of their voting rights until the 1960s.

Harrison lost another bill designed to provide federal funds for students in needy communities, especially in the teaching of reading. The bill, sponsored by Senator Henry Blair, had failed in 1880 and again in 1884. When it was introduced in the Senate in 1890, it caused six weeks of bitter debate, then went down to defeat. Some opponents voted against the bill because they feared federal

"Czar" Thomas B. Reed, Speaker of the House, was a powerful congressional Republican who often ignored or opposed the president's recommendations.

Wounded Knee

In the 1880s, many Native Americans in the Great Plains were swept up by the Ghost Dance religion. This wave of religious feeling suggested that Native Americans could bring about the destruction of the existing world and create an eternal paradise for their people by praying, chanting, and dancing. Some Ghost Dance believers spoke of a war with American authorities in order to bring about this new world, and officers of U.S. troops stationed in the West became concerned.

On December 29, 1890, American soldiers attacked an Indian camp near Wounded Knee Creek in South Dakota, killing 146, including many women and children. In the fighting, 25 U.S. soldiers were killed. It was the last of more than 250 years' worth of "Indian wars" between European settlers and Native American tribes. Though Harrison supported the rights and education of Native Americans in general, millions of acres of Indian land were opened to white settlers during his administration.

☆ ☆ ☆

involvement in local schools. Others opposed it because it could obviously be used to benefit African American students in the South.

Harrison strongly and publicly supported the Blair bill, even though Republican leaders warned him that congressional support for it was not strong. He deeply believed that Republicans should unite to support the rights of African Americans, but he was unable to persuade Congress to act.

The Billion-Dollar Congress of and the Election 1890

Even after debating the major bills listed above, the Congress of 1889–90 had time to appropriate so much money that it became known as the "billion-dollar Congress." It broadened the qualifications for veterans' pensions, leading to a huge increase in government payments; appropriated large sums to support steamship companies and new railroads; and spent large sums for the construction of new U.S. navy ships. Before the session was over, the Congress became the first to appropriate $1 billion.

These huge expenditures, along with the emotional dispute over the tariff, created a firestorm among Democrats. In the 1890 congressional elections, Democrats warned that Republicans were spending the country into ruin and that the new high tariffs were sure to drive up prices. More than 90 percent of voters went to the polls, and the Democrats scored a major victory. They gained a majority in the House of Representatives and also narrowed the Republican majority in the Senate. Harrison knew he would get little cooperation from the House in the second half of his term. In fact, the House tried to repeal, or undo, laws passed by the last Congress, but was thwarted by the Senate.

The free-spending billion-dollar Congress would cause Republicans difficulty in coming elections, but much of the money was used for constructive purposes. It paid for river and harbor improvements around the country. Perhaps most important, a large appropriation went to improving the U.S. Navy. During Harrison's term, the navy would leapfrog out of the Civil War era and prepare the United States for its international role in the 20th century.

Chapter 5

Personal Tragedies ——————————

In the second half of Harrison's administration, attention turned away from Congress and toward foreign affairs. President Harrison had expected to receive strong support in dealing with overseas matters from his secretary of state, James Blaine. Unfortunately, Blaine had been suffering from serious illness and had been struck by a series of personal tragedies.

In fact, Harrison's administration had been besieged by tragic accidents and illness. His secretary, Elijah Halford, collapsed from overwork and illness in 1889. At first, Halford was too ill to be moved. Harrison arranged for necessary surgery to be performed in the White House and allowed Mrs. Halford to stay there while her husband recuperated. In 1890, Navy Secretary Benjamin Tracy lost his wife and daughter in a house fire in 1890 and was seriously injured himself. Once again, Harrison arranged for Tracy to stay at the White House while he recuperated. Treasury Secretary William Windom died halfway through Harrison's term.

During this time, Blaine suffered two tragic blows. In January 1890, his son Walker Blaine, who served as an assistant to his father, died of pneumonia. Three weeks later, Blaine's daughter died. Later, in 1892, another of his sons would die. Devastated by these losses and by his own ill health, Blaine was absent from his duties for long periods. President Harrison stepped in and conducted his own foreign policy.

The Navy and National Defense

Even before Harrison was elected, the attention of the United States was turning to questions of national defense. Great Britain and other European powers were assembling worldwide empires through the use of powerful navies and the activities of their merchants and traders. By contrast, the United States had been concentrating on its own affairs at home, and had paid little attention to its defenses or to its navy.

President Chester Arthur had taken the first steps toward building a modern navy before Harrison became president. Now Harrison worked with his navy secretary, Benjamin Tracy, to speed up the expensive job of building a modern fleet to protect American interests in the world.

The Navy Department had studied Great Britain's powerful navy and knew that its newest ships were made of a special strong nickel-steel alloy. Secretary Tracy worked with steel tycoon Andrew Carnegie to create the same alloy for new ships for the U.S. navy. Carnegie delivered, and with funds appropriated by Congress, the navy strengthened its fleet with new steel warships. During Harrison's term of office, the U.S. navy rose from twelfth strongest in the world to sixth.

Haiti, Central America, and Hawaii ——————

Harrison knew that to be effective, the navy would need friendly ports and coaling stations (for refueling) in the waters surrounding its borders. During his administration, he tried to negotiate the rights to set up a naval base in the island nation of Haiti to help patrol the Caribbean. The Haitian government refused his proposal, however, and he was unwilling to use force to accomplish his aim.

The navy was also deeply interested in creating a passage from the Atlantic to the Pacific Oceans through Central America so that it could move its ships easily to patrol both regions. Through the 1880s, a French company was hard at work to build a canal through Panama, but in 1889, only a month before Harrison took office, the company went bankrupt. Naval officials and U.S. commercial interests hoped that the United States could take over the work of building the canal, but the French refinanced the company and continued working. The canal remained unfinished through Harrison's term.

In the meantime, Harrison also worked toward establishing a naval base in the Hawaiian Islands, 2,000 miles (3,200 km) southwest of California in the Pacific. The islands were ruled by Queen Liliuokalani, but the economy of the islands was controlled by a group of non-Hawaiian plantation owners. In 1893, during Harrison's last weeks as president, the planters forced the queen to give up her power, and they established a new government. They received support from the U.S. consul, and U.S. marines were landed "to help keep order." Harrison immediately submitted to the Senate a treaty to *annex* Hawaii, making it a possession of the United States. The Senate did not act, however, and incoming president Grover Cleveland withdrew the treaty and urged the new government in Hawaii to return Queen Liliuokalani to the throne. The government refused to step down, however. Five years later, in 1898, the United States annexed the islands.

Sanford Dole, the son of mainland missionaries to Hawaii, became Hawaii's president after U.S. planters deposed Queen Liliuokalani. Dole later established pineapple plantations on the islands, and his name is still associated with that tropical fruit.

Europe and South America

In 1891, Harrison's administration faced a crisis in trade policy with Germany and France. The countries had been restricting imports of U.S. pork, claiming that it was infected with a pest that causes the disease trichinosis. In reality, they were trying to protect their own farmers, whose pork products were more expensive. In order to end the restrictions, Harrison took two steps. First, he supported a new meat inspection act to assure that U.S. pork was not a carrier of trichinosis. Then he warned Germany that the sugar it exported to the United States could easily be replaced by sugar from Cuba. In a major success for Harrison, Germany agreed to give up its ban on U.S. pork, and by the end of 1891 other European nations followed.

A second international incident involved Chile, a nation on the Pacific shore of South America. Chileans were still angry with the United States for siding against their country in their war with Peru and Bolivia nearly ten years earlier. Then in 1891, the United States supported Chile's president against a rebellion that began in the Chilean congress. The U.S. minister in Chile helped protect the president and other government officials against attacks by the rebels. In February a U.S. warship anchored off the coast. Rebels won control of the government anyway. Then in October, some U.S. sailors came ashore. They got into a dispute with rebel supporters and two of them were killed. U.S. officials demanded an investigation, but nothing happened.

As the United States made plans for military action against Chile, the new government finally issued an apology for the deaths of the sailors and agreed to pay $75,000 in damages. Even Theodore Roosevelt, usually a critic of Harrison, praised the president's strong handling of the Chilean situation.

Canada and Great Britain

Harrison also helped resolve a long-simmering dispute with Canada. Canadian hunters were intensively hunting seals in the waters of the Bering Sea off the coast of Alaska. The United States claimed that they were capturing seals that Alaskan hunters would otherwise have captured on land. The U.S. navy began seizing the Canadian ships in the region. In retaliation, Canada began seizing U.S. fishermen in waters off Canada's Atlantic coast.

In 1891 Great Britain interceded on behalf of Canada and sent warships to the Bering Sea. Harrison agreed to submit the dispute to *arbitration*. The issue was finally settled in 1893. The arbitrators ruled that the United States had no property rights to seals in international waters and required it to pay damages to Canada for seizing ships. On the other hand, they also ruled that seals could not be hunted within 60 miles (96 km) of Alaska's Pribilof Islands and limited the time of year Canadians could hunt seals. This ruling providing protection to American seal hunters and ended the dispute.

Coming from their spacious and comfortable Indianapolis home, the Harrisons found that living in the White House was not a treat. The president and his wife arrived with both of their adult children and their families. They soon found living quarters cramped, and the rooms arranged haphazardly, many of them close to offices where outsiders came to work.

Carrie Harrison proposed the construction of a complete new wing for the White House, which would include spacious new living quarters for a president's family. Congress turned down her grandiose plan, but appropriated $35,000 (then a large sum) for repairs and improvements. One of the most vexing problems was rats. A rat even killed a caged canary during Grover Cleveland's second term in office! The Harrisons were the first White House occupants to have electricity, but they were nervous about turning off light switches—a butler did that for them.

Caroline Scott Harrison (above) as first lady. She helped refurbish the White House and made plans for new landscaping and gardens. The photo on the facing page shows the White House Blue Room, which she redecorated.

☆ ★ ☆

A New Election Season

In April 1891 Harrison had begun an extensive five-week trip around the United States, covering 9,200 miles (14,800 km) and visiting all regions of the country. He was met with great acclaim and seemed to be leading a popular administration. But in Washington, the administration was at a standstill. Democratic victories in the 1890 congressional elections had put Harrison and his government on the defensive. It could not pass new initiatives in Congress and had to fight to preserve its earlier accomplishments. By 1892, public opinion turned against the administration.

As presidential elections neared, Harrison seemed less than eager to run for another term. While walking in Washington with a friend one day, he pointed to the White House and said, "There is my jail." Harrison's problems were not only with Democrats. Republican leaders resented his unwillingness to take advice. Even James G. Blaine, who had been ill for much of Harrison's term, recovered enough to consider running again for president. Only when Harrison realized that the party wanted to dump him and run someone else did he dig in his heels and announce that he would be a candidate. When Harrison told his wife his decision, she asked, "Why, General? Why, when it has been so hard for you?"

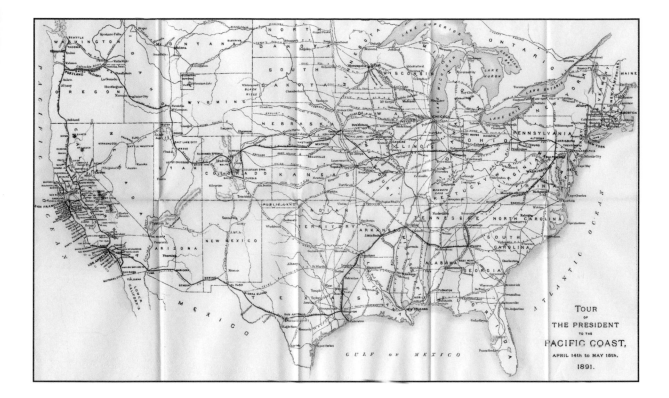

In the spring of 1891, Benjamin Harrison made the most ambitious tour of the country of any president to that time. He traveled 9,200 miles (mostly by train) and gave 104 speeches.

Harrison imposed his authority as president and leader of the party, and gained the Republican nomination on the first ballot. Getting elected proved to be a more difficult problem. Many Republicans were only lukewarm about his candidacy and sat on their hands through the campaign, offering only token support.

In 1892, Grover Cleveland (left) ran against President Harrison (right). It was the only time in U.S. history that a former president and a current president ran against each other.

Then Harrison received a devastating personal blow. That summer, Carrie developed an active and dangerous case of tuberculosis. Harrison did not even mount an organized "front porch" campaign. Instead, he spent part of the summer with Carrie at their vacation home in the remote Adirondack Mountains, hoping the fresh mountain air would bring some improvement. Out of respect, Democratic candidate Grover Cleveland also gave up personal campaigning. By the time Harrison returned to Washington in September, it was clear that Carrie was dying. A reporter noted that Harrison's eyes were "red, from weeping" as he emerged from the train. Caroline Harrison died on October 25, less than two weeks before the election. Her funeral and burial took place in Indianapolis.

Harrison seemed to care little when he lost the election to Cleveland. He left Washington after Cleveland's inauguration in March and was greeted by a cheering crowd upon his return to Indianapolis. "I made no mistake in coming home at once," Harrison told his son later. "There are no friends like the old ones." With that, Harrison's political life was behind him.

Chapter 6

Back to Work

Back in Indianapolis in the spring of 1893, Benjamin Harrison took a well-deserved rest. "I find myself exceedingly lazy, unable yet to do much of any work," he wrote to his friend John Wanamaker. His daughter Mamie and her two children, Benjamin and Mary, spent much time with him at first, as they had during his last months in Washington. Harrison was especially close to his grandson Benjamin, whose high chair stood next to his grandfather's chair at the dinner table. The children's pet goat and burro were among the more unusual pets in Harrison's Indianapolis neighborhood.

After the break, Harrison went back to work, reestablishing his law firm and accepting only clients willing to make a first payment of $500. He also agreed to give six law lectures at the new Stanford University in California in 1894. For these lectures he received the huge sum of $25,000. They were later published as part

Berkeley Lodge

In 1895 Harrison returned to the Adirondacks, where he greatly enjoyed outdoor life, much as he had as a child. He decided to make his own home-away-from-home there, and called it Berkeley Lodge. It was named for the Virginia plantation home of his great-grandfather, the fifth Benjamin Harrison, signer of the Declaration of Independence.

☆ ★ ☆

of a book called *Views of an Ex-President*. For the first time in his adult life he was happy "not to be under the spur" of too much work pressure.

Meanwhile, the country was going through the most severe economic depression in its history. Only weeks after Harrison left office, the stock market crashed, and in the following months hundreds of companies went into bankruptcy. Workers were laid off, farm prices dropped, and suffering was widespread. Democrats claimed that the financial panic was caused by the high tariffs and the Silver Purchase Act passed during Harrison's administration. President Cleveland persuaded Congress to repeal the Silver Purchase Act, but the depression continued. In the end, Americans blamed Cleveland, not Harrison, for the hard economic times.

In December 1895 Harrison announced his engagement to Mary Lord Dimmick. A widow, she was a niece of Carrie Harrison and had helped care for

In 1896 Harrison married Mary Lord Dimmick, a niece of his first wife.

her during her long illness. Harrison wrote to his son Russell that a life alone is "a very lonely one and I cannot go on as now." Even so, Harrison's son and daughter were unhappy about their father's engagement and refused to attend the wedding. In February 1897, Mary Lord Harrison gave birth to a daughter. The couple named her Elizabeth after both of their mothers.

The Harrisons' daughter Elizabeth was born in 1897.

As the 1896 presidential election approached, newspapers began to mention Harrison as a possible candidate. After four years of hard times, they recalled his intelligence and experience, and reported that he seemed more likable than before. Harrison had no interest in running, however, and the Republican nomination went to William McKinley, sponsor of the famous tariff bill. Harrison did agree to be the keynote speaker at a Republican rally to kick off McKinley's campaign in New York. His speech, delivered with his usual compelling style, was well received and reprinted in newspapers around the country.

In 1898 Harrison was engaged by the government of Venezuela to represent it in a serious dispute with Great Britain over the boundary between Venezuela and British Guiana (the present-day country of Guyana). Harrison knew no Spanish and knew little about Venezuela, but he delved into the country's history and the background of the dispute. He was assisted by former navy secretary Benjamin Tracy and others, preparing to argue Venezuela's case before an arbitration court in Paris. Once again, Harrison buried himself in his work and soon began feeling overwhelmed and irritable. By February 1899, Harrison admitted, "I have felt recently as if I was on the verge of a breakdown. For one year now I have taken no rest."

He sailed to Europe with his family in May. In June, the trial began. Of the five arbiters, two were British, one was Russian, and two were American. Even

Benjamin Harrison during his retirement. He died in 1901, eight years after leaving the presidency.

though Venezuela had a strong case, the arbiters granted 90 percent of the disputed territory to British Guiana. Many believed that Venezuela was cheated in the trial, and Harrison felt he had failed. Years later, evidence was uncovered that the British judges and the Russian judge had conspired to throw the trial in British Guiana's favor, no matter what evidence was presented.

When Harrison returned home, he continued working, but at a slower pace. In 1900, he traveled to Yellowstone Park and then up to the Adirondacks. In March 1901 he came down with a cold, which turned to a serious case of pneumonia. His health failed rapidly, and he died at home in the afternoon of March 13, 1901, attended by Mary Harrison and the Reverend M. L. Haines, pastor of the First Presbyterian Church where Harrison had been a member for nearly half a century.

In its front-page obituary of Harrison the next day, the New York *Times* reported that "News of the death spread quickly through the city. . . . Within a few moments after the announcement of the death the flags on all the public buildings and most of the downtown business blocks were hoisted at half mast."

Harrison left an estate valued at about $400,000, most of which went to his wife and young daughter. He was still estranged from his son and older daughter, but left a modest trust fund for his grandchildren's education.

Legacy

For many years, Harrison was considered one of the least successful U.S. presidents, but scholars in recent years have begun to revise this judgment. The first two years of his term produced more legislation on important issues than many presidents produced in full terms of office. In addition, Harrison helped fashion a more active and engaged foreign policy, which would be continued under Republican presidents William McKinley and Theodore Roosevelt. In addition, Harrison was the only president for many years to come who took a strong stand on the rights of African Americans, even though he was unable to pass legislation to improve their situation.

Benjamin Harrison wasn't a strong leader, as interaction with people other than family or close friends was a skill he lacked. But, as Hoosier poet James Whitcomb Riley said of him at his death, "above everything else Harrison was fearless and just."

Fast Facts | Benjamin Harrison

Birth:	August 20, 1833
Birthplace:	North Bend, Ohio
Parents:	John Scott and Elizabeth Irwin Harrison
Sisters & Brothers:	*Half sisters*
	Elizabeth "Bessie" Short (1825–1904)
	Sarah "Sallie" Lucretia (1829–?)
	Full brothers and sisters
	Archibald Irwin (1832–1870)
	Mary Jane "Jennie" (1835–1867)
	Carter Bassett (1840–1905)
	Anna Symmes II (1842–1926)
	John Scott (1844–1926)
	(four other children died in infancy)
Education:	Miami University, Oxford, Ohio, graduated 1852
Occupation:	Lawyer
Marriage:	To Caroline "Carrie" Scott (1832–1892), October 20, 1853
	To Mary Lord Dimmick (1858–1948), April 6, 1896
Children:	*With Caroline Harrison*
	Russell (1854–1936)
	Mary "Mamie" (1858–1930)
	With Mary Lord Harrison
	Elizabeth (1897–1955)
Political Party:	Republican
Public Offices:	1861–1862 Indiana Supreme Court Reporter
	1865–1866 Indiana Supreme Court Reporter
	1881–1887 United States Senator from Indiana
	1889–1893 23rd President of the United States
His Vice President:	Levi P. Morton
Major Actions as President:	1890 Signed major legislation dealing with the tariff, trusts, and currency
	1891 Reopened European markets for American pork producers
	Managed a serious conflict with Chile
	Contributed to modernizing the U.S. Navy
Death:	March 13, 1901
Age at Death:	67 years
Burial Place:	Crown Hill Cemetery , Indianapolis, Indiana

Caroline Lavinia Scott Harrison

Birth:	October 1, 1832
Birthplace:	Oxford, Ohio
Parents:	The Reverend Dr. John W. Scott and Mary Potts Neal Scott
Sisters & Brothers:	Elizabeth Lord
	Mary Spears
	John
	Henry
Education:	Oxford Female Institute, Oxford, Ohio
Marriage:	To Benjamin Harrison, October 20, 1853
Children:	Russell (1854–1936)
	Mary "Mamie" (1858–1930)
Firsts:	Installed first holiday Christmas tree in the White House
	Established tradition that each administration should contribute a pattern to the White House china
	Helped raise funds for the Johns Hopkins University Medical School on condition that it admit women
Death:	October 25, 1892
Age at Death:	60 years
Burial Place:	Crown Hill Cemetery, Indianapolis, Indiana

Timeline

1833	1840	1841	1852	1853
Benjamin Harrison is born in North Bend, Ohio, August 20	William Henry Harrison is elected ninth president of the United States	William Henry Harrison dies one month after taking office, April 4	Benjamin Harrison graduates from Miami University, Oxford, Ohio	Harrison and Caroline "Carrie" Scott are married in Oxford, Ohio

1864	1865	1876	1879	1881
Receives commendation and promotion to brigadier general for bravery at battles of Resaca and Peach Tree Creek, Georgia	Mustered out of Union army at war's end, returns to Indianapolis	Runs as last-minute nominee for governor of Indiana, loses by 5,000 votes	Appointed to Mississippi River Commission by President Rutherford B. Hayes	Elected U.S. senator by Indiana state legislature

1892	1894	1896	1897	1899
Nominated by Republicans for re-election, June; Carrie Harrison dies of tuberculosis, October 25; Harrison defeated by Democrat Grover Cleveland, November	Gives series of law lectures at newly established Stanford University in California	Marries Mary Lord Dimmick, a niece of his first wife	Daughter Elizabeth is born	Represents Venezuela in a boundary dispute against Great Britain, arguing before an international arbitration panel in Paris

1854

Harrison is licensed to practice law; he and Carrie move to Indianapolis, Indiana; their first child, Russell, is born

1858

Daughter Mary ("Mamie") is born

1860

Benjamin Harrison elected state supreme court reporter; Abraham Lincoln elected president

1861

Confederate troops fire on Fort Sumter in South Carolina, beginning the U.S. Civil War, April 12

1862

Harrison enlists in Union army, takes command of 70th Indiana regiment

1887

Defeated for a second term in the Senate

1888

Nominated as Republican candidate for president, June; defeats Democrat Grover Cleveland in fall election

1889

Inaugurated as 23rd president, March

1890

Signs Sherman Antitrust Act, Sherman Silver Purchase Act, and McKinley Tariff Act, all passed by the "billion-dollar Congress"

1892

Resolves standoff with Chile over death of American sailors

1901

Benjamin Harrison dies at age 67, March 13

Glossary

★ ★ ★ ★ ★

abolitionists: in the United States before 1865, a group that advocated abolishing, or completely ending, slavery

annex: to add a region to an existing nation or state; Hawaii was annexed by the United States in 1898

arbitration: a means of settling a dispute between individuals or governments in which neutral parties called arbitrators listen to both sides and make a decision

ballot: a vote, especially at a political convention; if no candidate wins the required majority on the first ballot, the convention votes again and again until one candidate wins

cabinet: the secretaries (or directors) of government departments, who gather to advise the president

federal: in the United States, having to do with the national or central government, as opposed to state or local government

filibuster: in U.S. politics, to refuse to end debate and bring a bill to a vote; used by opponents of the bill to keep it from passing

prosecutor: a lawyer who brings government charges against persons accused of committing a crime

secede: to withdraw a government unit from a larger government; the southern states seceded from the United States before the Civil War

tariff: a tax on goods imported into a country for sale

trust: a group of related businesses owned and controlled by a single small group to gain business advantages

Further Reading

★ ★ ★ ★ ★

Francis, Sandra. *Benjamin Harrison: Our Twenty-third President*. Chanhassan, MN: Child's World, 2002.

Mayo, Edith. *The Smithsonian Book of the First Ladies: Their Lives, Times, and Issues*. New York: Henry Holt, 1996.

Smith, C. Carter. *Presidents of a Growing Country: A Sourcebook on the U.S. Presidency*. Brookfield, CT: Millbrook Press, 1993.

MORE ADVANCED READING

DeGregorio, William. *Complete Book of U.S. Presidents*. Fort Lee, NJ: Barricade, 2001.

Socolofsky, Homer E., and Allan B. Spetter. *The Presidency of Benjamin Harrison*. Lawrence: University Press of Kansas, 1987.

Places to Visit

★ ★ ★ ★ ★ ★

President Benjamin Harrison Home
1230 North Delaware Street
Indianapolis, IN 46202
(317) 631-1888
www.presidentbenjaminharrison.org/

The President Benjamin Harrison Home,
President Harrison's Indianapolis residence,
is today a museum dedicated to his life. The
home has been restored and contains many
artifacts that belonged to the Harrison family. The home also houses a library for
research on the life and times of Benjamin
Harrison.

The White House
1600 Pennsylvania Avenue NW
Washington, DC 20500
Visitors' Office: (202) 456-7041
http://www.whitehouse.gov

Benjamin Harrison's home from 1889 to
1893. Caroline Harrison supervised many
improvements in the building and organized
the White House china collection.

Online Sites of Interest

★ **The Benjamin Harrison Home**

http://www.presidentbenjaminharrison.org

This site, operated by the Harrison museum and library in Indianapolis, provides a useful biography of Harrison and additional information on his family.

★ **The American Presidency**

http://gi.grolier.com/presidents

This site provides biographical information on the presidents at different reading levels, based on material in Scholastic/Grolier encyclopedias.

★ **The American President**

http://www.americanpresident.org

Provides valuable information on the life and times of U.S. presidents. Originally prepared from material for a public television series on the president, the site is now managed by the University of Virginia.

★ **Internet Public Library, Presidents of the United States (IPL POTUS)**

http://www.ipl.org/div/potus/bharrison.html

Includes concise information about Harrison and his presidency and provides links to other sites of interest.

★ **The White House**

http://www.whitehouse.gov/history/presidents/bh23.html

Offers a brief biographical article on Benjamin Harrison. Other addresses at this site provide additional information about the White House and its history.

Table of Presidents

	1. George Washington	2. John Adams	3. Thomas Jefferson	4. James Madison
Took office	Apr 30 1789	Mar 4 1797	Mar 4 1801	Mar 4 1809
Left office	Mar 3 1797	Mar 3 1801	Mar 3 1809	Mar 3 1817
Birthplace	Westmoreland Co, VA	Braintree, MA	Shadwell, VA	Port Conway, VA
Birth date	Feb 22 1732	Oct 20 1735	Apr 13 1743	Mar 16 1751
Death date	Dec 14 1799	July 4 1826	July 4 1826	June 28 1836

	9. William H. Harrison	10. John Tyler	11. James K. Polk	12. Zachary Taylor
Took office	Mar 4 1841	Apr 6 1841	Mar 4 1845	Mar 5 1849
Left office	**Apr 4 1841•**	Mar 3 1845	Mar 3 1849	**July 9 1850•**
Birthplace	Berkeley, VA	Greenway, VA	Mecklenburg Co, NC	Barboursville, VA
Birth date	Feb 9 1773	Mar 29 1790	Nov 2 1795	Nov 24 1784
Death date	Apr 4 1841	Jan 18 1862	June 15 1849	July 9 1850

	17. Andrew Johnson	18. Ulysses S. Grant	19. Rutherford B. Hayes	20. James A. Garfield
Took office	Apr 15 1865	Mar 4 1869	Mar 5 1877	Mar 4 1881
Left office	Mar 3 1869	Mar 3 1877	Mar 3 1881	**Sept 19 1881•**
Birthplace	Raleigh, NC	Point Pleasant, OH	Delaware, OH	Orange, OH
Birth date	Dec 29 1808	Apr 27 1822	Oct 4 1822	Nov 19 1831
Death date	July 31 1875	July 23 1885	Jan 17 1893	Sept 19 1881

5. James Monroe	6. John Quincy Adams	7. Andrew Jackson	8. Martin Van Buren
Mar 4 1817	Mar 4 1825	Mar 4 1829	Mar 4 1837
Mar 3 1825	Mar 3 1829	Mar 3 1837	Mar 3 1841
Westmoreland Co, VA	Braintree, MA	The Waxhaws, SC	Kinderhook, NY
Apr 28 1758	July 11 1767	Mar 15 1767	Dec 5 1782
July 4 1831	Feb 23 1848	June 8 1845	July 24 1862

13. Millard Fillmore	14. Franklin Pierce	15. James Buchanan	16. Abraham Lincoln
July 9 1850	Mar 4 1853	Mar 4 1857	Mar 4 1861
Mar 3 1853	Mar 3 1857	Mar 3 1861	**Apr 15 1865•**
Locke Township, NY	Hillsborough, NH	Cove Gap, PA	Hardin Co, KY
Jan 7 1800	Nov 23 1804	Apr 23 1791	Feb 12 1809
Mar 8 1874	Oct 8 1869	June 1 1868	Apr 15 1865

21. Chester A. Arthur	22. Grover Cleveland	23. Benjamin Harrison	24. Grover Cleveland
Sept 19 1881	Mar 4 1885	Mar 4 1889	Mar 4 1893
Mar 3 1885	Mar 3 1889	Mar 3 1893	Mar 3 1897
Fairfield, VT	Caldwell, NJ	North Bend, OH	Caldwell, NJ
Oct 5 1829	Mar 18 1837	Aug 20 1833	Mar 18 1837
Nov 18 1886	June 24 1908	Mar 13 1901	June 24 1908

25. William McKinley

Took office	Mar 4 1897
Left office	**Sept 14 1901•**
Birthplace	Niles, OH
Birth date	Jan 29 1843
Death date	Sept 14 1901

26. Theodore Roosevelt

Sept 14 1901
Mar 3 1909
New York, NY
Oct 27 1858
Jan 6 1919

27. William H. Taft

Mar 4 1909
Mar 3 1913
Cincinnati, OH
Sept 15 1857
Mar 8 1930

28. Woodrow Wilson

Mar 4 1913
Mar 3 1921
Staunton, VA
Dec 28 1856
Feb 3 1924

33. Harry S. Truman

Took office	Apr 12 1945
Left office	Jan 20 1953
Birthplace	Lamar, MO
Birth date	May 8 1884
Death date	Dec 26 1972

34. Dwight D. Eisenhower

Jan 20 1953
Jan 20 1961
Denison, TX
Oct 14 1890
Mar 28 1969

35. John F. Kennedy

Jan 20 1961
Nov 22 1963•
Brookline, MA
May 29 1917
Nov 22 1963

36. Lyndon B. Johnson

Nov 22 1963
Jan 20 1969
Johnson City, TX
Aug 27 1908
Jan 22 1973

41. George Bush

Took office	Jan 20 1989
Left office	Jan 20 1993
Birthplace	Milton, MA
Birth date	June 12 1924
Death date	—

42. Bill Clinton

Jan 20 1993
Jan 20 2001
Hope, AR
Aug 19 1946
—

43. George W. Bush

Jan 20 2001
—
New Haven, CT
July 6 1946
—

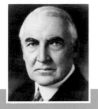

29. Warren G. Harding	**30. Calvin Coolidge**	**31. Herbert Hoover**	**32. Franklin D. Roosevelt**
Mar 4 1921	Aug 2 1923	Mar 4 1929	Mar 4 1933
Aug 2 1923•	Mar 3 1929	Mar 3 1933	**Apr 12 1945•**
Blooming Grove, OH	Plymouth, VT	West Branch, IA	Hyde Park, NY
Nov 21 1865	July 4 1872	Aug 10 1874	Jan 30 1882
Aug 2 1923	Jan 5 1933	Oct 20 1964	Apr 12 1945

37. Richard M. Nixon	**38. Gerald R. Ford**	**39. Jimmy Carter**	**40. Ronald Reagan**
Jan 20 1969	Aug 9 1974	Jan 20 1977	Jan 20 1981
Aug 9 1974★	Jan 20 1977	Jan 20 1981	Jan 20 1989
Yorba Linda, CA	Omaha, NE	Plains, GA	Tampico, IL
Jan 9 1913	July 14 1913	Oct 1 1924	Feb 6 1911
Apr 22 1994	—	—	June 5 2004

• Indicates the president died while in office.

★ Richard Nixon resigned before his term expired.

Index

Page numbers in *italics* indicate illustrations.

About the Author

Jean Kinney Williams has written many books for young readers, including a series on interesting American faiths, including *The Amish* and *The Quakers*. She lives in Cincinnati, Ohio, the city that Benjamin Harrison considered too dirty and noisy—but not far from North Bend, his childhood home.